Separation of Church and State

Irene Cumming Kleeberg

SEPARATION OF CHURCH AND STATE

Richard B. Morris, Consulting Editor

Franklin Watts   1986   A First Book
New York   London   Toronto   Sydney

Photographs courtesy of Culver Pictures, Inc.: p. 4;
AP/Wide World: pp. 9, 42, 43;
UPI/Bettmann Newsphotos: pp. 10, 28, 31, 46, 48, 54;
The Bettmann Archive: pp. 14, 16, 23, 34.

Library of Congress Cataloging-in-Publication Data

Kleeberg, Irene Cumming.
Separation of church and state.

(A First book)
Bibliography: p.
Includes index.
Summary: A history of the conflicts between the
government and religion in the United States, due to
interpretations of the Constitution. Also discusses
current on-going conflicts and recent Supreme Court
decisions.
1. Church and state—United States—Juvenile
literature. [1. Church and state] I. Morris, Richard
Brandon, 1904–   . II. Title.
BR516.K54   1986   322′.1′0973   85-31749
ISBN 0-531-10111-8

Contents

Separation of Church and State

Chapter

1

Separation of
Church and State

"Separation of church and state" is a phrase that is used so often many people think it is part of the United States Constitution. The words aren't, but the meaning is.

"Church" in this case doesn't mean any church or any particular religion. It means any religion at all (Christian, Jewish, Buddhist, Islamic, or any other religion, or even no religion). And "state" doesn't mean a state only in the sense that Vermont is a state, but all government. "Separation" is easier to figure out—it means "keeping apart."

The actual words establishing the separation of church and state in the United States come in three places in the Constitution—in Article II and Article VI and in Amendment I.

Article II, Section 1, Part 8 of the Constitution gives the oath of office for the president as "I do solemnly swear (or affirm) that I will faithfully execute the office of President of the United States, and will to the best of my ability preserve, protect, and defend the Constitution of the United States." By offering a choice of "swear" or "affirm" the writers of the Constitution made it possible for people with religious or other objections to swearing to become president.

In Article VI, Section 3, the Constitution says, "The Senators and Representatives before mentioned and the members of the several State legislatures, and all executive and judicial officers both of the United States and of the several states, shall be bound by oath or affirmation to support this Constitution; but no religious test shall ever be required as a qualification for public trust under the United States."

Two Key Amendments

Finally, and perhaps most importantly, in the First Amendment to the Constitution we find "Congress shall make no law respecting an establishment of religion, or prohibiting the free exercise thereof. . . ."

Note that the First Amendment says "Congress shall make no law"—it doesn't refer to the individual states or other types of government. The Fourteenth Amendment does refer to states—"No State shall make or enforce any law which shall abridge the privileges or immunities of citizens of the United States . . . nor deny to any person within its jurisdiction the equal protection of the laws"—and therefore it is often used with the First Amendment in cases, including "church and state" cases, involving states or municipalities.

It all seems very clear at first glance, but as times change and people change there have been many questions about what the Constitution means about religion (and many other subjects). The Constitution provides for final decisions on interpretation to be made by the Supreme Court.

The Supreme Court

How does it work? Here is a very simplified explanation.

Suppose someone believes something—a crèche (nativity scene) perhaps—in their town violates separation of church and state. The first, best, and least expensive (suing people is expensive) thing to do is ask to have it changed. If this doesn't work, the person could take the town or individuals to court, moving slowly from the lowest court to the Supreme Court, step by step.

If the Supreme Court refuses to hear the case (which often happens) the decision of the last court is binding, but if the Supreme Court hears the case its decision becomes the law. In this way the Constitution is "interpreted." People who don't like some of the Court's decisions say that in this way the Constitution is "changed."

Each time the Supreme Court makes a decision about "church and state," some people disagree with the decision. Some are really angry. But the decision stands unless it is later overturned by another Supreme Court decision—which is rare.

For Americans, living in a country with separation of church and state, this seems the right and natural way for things to be. Even the many Americans who would like to see a great deal more religion in the United States usually don't expect that one religion will be required for everyone. This is not true in many other countries. We'll talk about this later in the book.

Separation of church and state was not part of the reason most of the American colonies were settled. The settlers wanted freedom of religion, yes—but for themselves, rarely for anyone else. How did these colonies end up ratifying a Constitution and First Amendment guaranteeing such wide religious freedom?

A classic painting of early settlers going to church

Many questions remain to be considered concerning separation of church and state, and sooner or later the Supreme Court will probably be asked to consider many of them. We'll end up with some of the questions and various ways of looking at them.

Finally, we'll tell you where you can find more information, give you a glossary so you can check the meaning of words you aren't sure about, and an index to find things fast.

Chapter

2

The Constitution and the Supreme Court

The United States Constitution is the world's oldest written constitution. What is a constitution? How did we come to have one?

The original leaders of our country believed that a written constitution was needed to present a clear outline of government. Some believed that if Britain had had a written constitution (it still doesn't), it would have avoided trouble with the colonies.

The Preamble to the Constitution explains why it was written: "We the People of the United States, in order to form a more perfect union, establish justice, insure domestic tranquility, provide for the common defense, promote the general welfare, and secure the blessings of liberty to ourselves and our posterity, do ordain and establish this Constitution for the United States of America."

A constitution is like the rules for a club—it sets up from the beginning how various matters are to be handled. Amendments are sections added onto the original Constitution.

When the Constitution was ratified, many of the states ratifying it suggested amendments, especially ones spelling out the rights of citizens. As a result twelve amendments were sent to the states in 1789. Ten of those amendments were ratified by 1791.

These first ten amendments to the Constitution are called the Bill of Rights. The first nine protect individual liberty; the tenth emphasizes that powers not specifically given to Congress remain with the states or the people. The two amendments that didn't pass had to do with the apportionment of congressional representatives and salaries for Congress.

There are two sections to the religion part of the First Amendment, and even Supreme Court justices when writing about them refer to them with a kind of shorthand. One clause is the "establishment" clause—that's the one about "Congress shall make no law respecting an establishment of religion." The other clause is the "free exercise" clause forbidding Congress from making laws prohibiting the free exercise of religion.

Thomas Jefferson is credited with the phrase "wall of separation" to describe the relationship between church and state in the First Amendment. "Church" means any religion and "state" means any government, not just the individual states.

It all seems pretty clear, doesn't it? The government of the United States, at whatever level, was neither to help any religion nor to hinder it.

However, over the years the "wall" has been almost like a movable wall on a stage in a theater, moving one way, then another way, then back the first way. And since the Supreme Court is the final court for deciding whether or not things are constitutional, the Supreme Court, by its decisions, pushes and pulls that wall back and forth.

In the News

Separation of church and state has been in the news a great deal recently. Why? Here are some possible reasons:

The United States Supreme Court in 1986

FUNK'S

CLOSED SUNDAY
GONE TO
CHUCRH

FUNK'S
FOOD CIT
PARKIN

KRUSOE

1. The decline in membership of religious groups. For many people nothing is more important than their religion. They may believe that their religion is not only right for them but also right for everyone. As membership in religious organizations has dropped recently, these people worry that this will hurt the United States. They blame this decline on recent Supreme Court decisions concerning "church and state," particularly ones such as that concerning prayer in the schools.

2. Changing morals. Morals are standards of "good" and "evil." Usually morals change so slowly (sometimes to less strict, sometimes to more strict) that the change is almost unnoticed. In the past thirty or forty years, however, morals have changed so very rapidly to less strict that almost everyone is aware of the changes— whether or not they are in favor of them. Morals skirt the edges of religion and usually deal with smaller questions than most religion does, but many people feel that such Supreme Court decisions as those dealing with Sunday work have affected morals.

3. A more litigious society. This means that there are more lawyers around and more people prepared to go to court for what they think is right. There is also a tendency for public interest organizations to support court cases on one side or the other.

4. A changing Supreme Court. The Supreme Court interprets the Constitution and its amendments. There are nine Supreme Court justices who are appointed for life (or until they resign). They are appointed by the president as a vacancy occurs. Presidents appoint justices they believe will reflect their point of view. Courts

The owners of Funk's announce that
they have gone to church.

are usually considered either liberal or conservative, depending on the majority of justices. (In American politics, the term *liberal* is used to describe a group that strongly favors individual freedom and social reform; the term *conservative* is used to describe a group that wants to keep things as they are.) In 1985 the Court was considered conservative. However, liberal decisions are often made by conservative Courts and conservative decisions by liberal Courts. Decisions made by one Court are occasionally overturned by another, later Court.

5. The school prayer decision by the Supreme Court in 1962. Up until this case most public schools in the United States started each day with what were called Opening Exercises. They included the salute to the flag, a patriotic song, a chapter from the Bible, and a prayer.

When the Court decided that prayers and Bible reading violated the First Amendment, even many people who agreed were surprised. Many of the "church and state" cases at all levels of the courts that have come up recently are related in one way or another to this decision.

Chapter

3

Church and State
in the New World

If someone were to ask you, "Why did the Pilgrims come to America?" what would your answer be?

If you answered "for freedom of religion" or "to worship God as they saw fit" you would be right. In fact, America wasn't the first place the Pilgrims tried. They first went to Leiden in the Netherlands for this freedom (the Dutch have traditionally been extremely tolerant of other people's religions.)

After about ten years in Leiden, anxious to live away from other people not of their culture, they sailed (on their ship, the *Mayflower*) to the New World. They had permission to settle in Virginia, but landed instead in Massachusetts in 1620. The Pilgrims got permission to stay at Plymouth, where they set up a colony.

Massachusetts Bay Colony
and Rhode Island: Two Different
Views of Religion

Ten years later (1630), the Puritans came from England to America and organized the Massachusetts Bay Colony. The Puritans were

members of the Church of England who wanted to reform, or purify, the practices of the church. The colony was based on freedom of religion—but from a very limited point of view.

No one was allowed to vote, for instance, who was not a member of the church. In fact, people who even questioned the church had a difficult time. Roger Williams was forced to leave the colony because he taught that political leaders had no authority over religious matters and that people had the right to worship God as their consciences dictated. He went to Rhode Island in 1635, bought land from the Indians, and found a place of refuge from religious persecution.

Eventually he obtained a patent (later, in 1663, a royal charter) giving the land he settled complete liberty of conscience. One example of his tolerance: he let a group of Quakers settle in Rhode Island even though he himself thought their ideas were sinfully wrong.

Another exile from Massachusetts was Anne Hutchinson. She was forced to leave the colony because she held informal meetings to talk about the sermons that had been given the previous Sunday. She also ran into trouble over her idea that only faith—belief in God—was needed for a person to enter heaven; the church believed that good works were also needed. She was tried by the General Court and sentenced to banishment. In 1637, she and her family went to Rhode Island.

*Ten years after the Pilgrims
landed in 1620, the Puritans
arrived on the* Arbella
at Salem, Massachusetts.

What the Puritans in the Massachusetts Bay Colony wanted was freedom of religion—but only for themselves. Anyone who disagreed with the religious beliefs of the community had to change his or her mind and repent or leave.

Other Colonies

Massachusetts wasn't the only place where one had to believe in a certain religion or leave. In Maryland, Lord Calvert (also called Lord Baltimore) established a community where Roman Catholics could find refuge (he was a Roman Catholic) and all other Christian sects except Unitarians were allowed to settle. This policy lasted about twenty years.

Gradually, more and more Puritans moved into the colony and gained control. Once in power, they banned Roman Catholics and the Church of England. In 1688, however, the Church of England was dominant in England and became the established religion and the established church of Maryland. An established religion means one religion is the religion of a nation or an area by law.

In fact, in nine of the colonies later to become states there was a belief that religion was part of government. The idea of an established religion still exists in many parts of the world.

The belief that one religion has the right answers to all the questions of life, including government, and the firm belief that people who don't agree with the religion are wrong and possibly wicked had certain results in the colonies.

*Anne Hutchinson preaching
in her house in Boston*

One result was that the churches were supported by taxes. Also, in some places only certain religions could hold religious meetings. Among other results were that only members of the religion could vote or hold office, only ministers of the religion could marry people to each other or bury the dead, and so forth.

Not all people who lived in a colony where their religion was forbidden left the area. Some people stayed, but they joined the dominant religion.

This then is the background against which the United States Constitution was written. To repeat, the United States Constitution is the oldest written constitution in the world. It has proved a model for the constitutions of many nations. It is an extremely flexible constitution and nowhere more so than in its view of the relationship between church and state.

How did it happen that a nation with a background of such strong religious feeling was able to write and ratify such a constitution?

Chapter

4

Moving Toward
Religious Freedom

When delegates from the new United States met to work on the Constitution, the majority of the states had some form of established religion. The Church of England (later called the Episcopal or Anglican Church) was the established church in most of the Southern colonies. The established church in much of New England was the one that grew out of the Puritan community—the Congregationalist Church.

Many of these colonies and some of the colonies that didn't have established religions had religious requirements for people wanting to hold office or vote.

How could these requirements be made in a society that believed in separation of church and state?

"Congress Shall Make . . ."

Look at the First Amendment again. It says "Congress shall make no law. . . ." It doesn't say the states couldn't make such laws.

Nevertheless, keeping in mind the fact that many of the states were founded on religious grounds, why were the authors of the

Constitution willing to write a constitution so in favor of separation of church and state?

The men who wrote the Constitution were not all of one religion and believed in various types of religious thought. Then, too, the Congregationalists of New England didn't want to risk losing the religious freedom (or dominance) they already had, any more than the Church of England in the South wanted to give up its freedom of religion (or dominance). Compromise was essential.

Great Changes
Shape the Nation

In any case, great changes had taken place in the nation since the first settlers arrived. Between 1620, when the Pilgrims landed, and 1787, when the Constitution was drawn up, the country had advanced tremendously.

Settlements were much more likely to be successful and survive than the early settlements were. Later settlers were better prepared for life in a new land, and they could count on receiving some help from the older, more established settlements.

The biggest change in the nation, though, was the size of the population. In 1620, the non-Indian population of what is now the United States was about 500. By 1776 the population was about 2,500,000. The colonies had grown! And, as a result, the colonists were no longer isolated from each other.

Various services brought the colonists together. A mail service of post riders went from Portsmouth, New Hampshire, into Virginia by 1732. Forty-three years later, in 1775, a more formal Post Office Department was set up. Although it might take months for a letter to travel from Massachusetts to Virginia, any mail service at all was a great advance.

Roads also helped create a nation. By 1756 stage coaches could make the trip between New York and Philadelphia in three days. By 1788 there were 2,000 miles (3,200 kilometers) of post roads running from New Hampshire to Georgia.

Other Factors

There were other elements that influenced both the leaders of the American Revolution and the authors of the Constitution. Pamphlets and newspapers were being issued in the colonies, and they influenced opinion.

The population was no longer as involved in religion as it had been during early colonial times. Life no longer consisted only of a struggle to live. There was time for people to read, think, and talk about ideas for living. And many of the new settlers as well as the descendants of the old settlers, while still religious, were more willing to accept other ideas.

Education, too, played a role in the growing tolerance. First of all, education became more important and more widely available. Colleges were founded—nine before the Revolution, including Columbia (originally King's College), Yale, and Princeton (originally the College of New Jersey). Most of these colleges were founded by Protestant religious groups with the aim of training ministers.

Although these colleges were often started with a religious purpose, they ended up educating young men (young women didn't get to go to college then) to think for themselves and to understand ideas about government that had existed among the ancient Greeks and Romans.

Even the Great Awakening—a series of religious meetings to revive faith in God, which swept the colonies in the period after about 1730—created a desire for more democratic institutions in religion.

Reasons for Settling Change, Too

Although some settlers had always come to the colonies for financial opportunity rather than for religious freedom, more and more settlers now came to the United States for a better chance.

Many settlers came to start a business of their own in a city or find a large farm with fertile soil. Others wanted a chance to get ahead without having to worry about class, title, or wealth.

Rules About Religion
and Government Soften

Although many colonies had established churches, the rules concerning the relationship between the church, the government, and the people were softening.

In Virginia, for instance, where the Church of England was the established church, so many Presbyterians (Church of Scotland) came into the area that while the laws concerning religion still existed they were rarely enforced. Then, too, important leaders, including Thomas Jefferson and James Madison, were opposed to the continuation of the established church of Virginia. Never-

In 1785 Thomas Jefferson's "Bill for Establishing Religious Freedom' was passed in Virginia.

theless, when the United States was formed, Virginia kept its established religion.

So did a majority of the other states. Massachusetts, which had had the Church of England as the established church for a time, had returned to the Congregational Church by the time of the Revolution. Connecticut and New Hampshire also had an established Congregational Church.

In some states, establishment of an official church had been one of those things that were more or less ignored. States such as Georgia, Maryland, and North and South Carolina felt a degree of indifference to the church, and separation came early and fairly easily. In Virginia there was more of a fight. Finally, James Madison led the passage of Thomas Jefferson's "Bill for Establishing Religious Freedom" in 1785.

As might be expected, since it was the Pilgrims and Puritans who led the movement to the colonies for religious freedom, states where the Congregationalist Church was established were much more stubborn. The Church was disestablished, that is, deprived of its established status and privileges, only as a result of a more liberal mood in the Church itself and outside the Church. Connecticut disestablished the Church in 1818, New Hampshire in 1819, and Massachusetts in 1833.

Why were these states allowed to have established religions so long?

The First Amendment, remember, says "Congress shall make no law respecting an establishment of religion or prohibiting the free exercise thereof. . . ." Some historians believe the words "Congress shall make no law" were used so states which already had established churches would not be forced to change them.

It should be remembered, however, that throughout the Constitution as much power as possible is reserved for the states and the people, with only enumerated power, that is, only those powers granted by the Constitution itself, going to the federal government.

The Fourteenth Amendment

Today, a state could not establish a religion. This is because of the Fourteenth Amendment to the Constitution, which was ratified in 1868. This is one of the "Civil War Amendments," which were designed to punish the South for leaving the union. They are now used to extend and define the Constitution. The Supreme Court, by holding that the Fourteenth Amendment made the First Amendment applicable to the states, greatly extended the concept of separation of church and state. The Fourteenth Amendment reads, in part, "No State shall make or enforce any law which shall abridge the privileges or immunities of citizens of the United States; nor shall any State deprive. . . ."

Chapter

5

Church and State
Throughout the World

Communist Countries
and Theocracies

True separation of church and state such as it exists in the United States is not usual in the rest of the world. Most communist countries (the Soviet Union, for instance) actively discourage religion; in some cases they forbid it.

A very different situation existed in Tibet. Before the Chinese imposed a new system in 1965, Tibet was a theocracy. It was ruled by religious leaders who believed they were guided by God.

The dalai lama, the ruler, and, second only to the ruler, a scholar, the panchen lama—considered direct reincarnations of their predecessors, who were reincarnations of Buddha—were the Tibetan leaders. Religion dominated every step of life in Tibet. There was little division, if any, between the religious and the political systems. Twenty percent of the population lived in lamaseries (similar to monasteries).

The Vatican—the residence of the pope, the leader of the Roman Catholic Church—is another example of a theocratic state.

An independent city-state surrounded by Rome, Italy, the Vatican issues its own money and stamps, and governs its own citizens. It has its own soldiers and flag. Government in the Vatican is headed by the pope and the law is canon law (the law of the church courts).

In many Islamic (Moslem) countries (such as some of the Arab states of the Middle East and northern Africa) the religion and the state merge to the point where the dividing line almost completely disappears. Islam influences everything, including not only religion and government but also how people get along together, how they reason, and what their art looks like.

In strict Islamic states only Moslems may be citizens. Courts make no distinction between religious and civic questions, and taxes support both the religion and the state. The belief is that the state and the religion are one. Since 1979, Iran has called itself an Islamic republic. Here, Islamic laws govern the nation and religious leaders hold complete power.

Other Countries

Most countries throughout the world are not nearly as extreme as either the communist countries or the theocracies. Most nations have worked out a relationship of one kind or another between church and state.

The dalai and panchen lamas pose in Peking with their "protector," Mao Zedong.

In England, Queen Elizabeth II is the head of the Church of England and in Scotland, the head of the Church of Scotland. She is more powerful over the Church of England; with the advice of the prime minister she appoints all the bishops.

The bishops sit and vote in the House of Lords, but the House of Commons must approve all changes in the Prayer Book. The Church of England is an extreme example of the role of the state in an established church.

There are many other relationships. In Finland, the state church is the Evangelical Lutheran Church, but the state also gives support to the Greek Orthodox Church.

In Brazil, which has a largely Roman Catholic population, the constitution requires separation of church and state. And in Mexico no religious group may own property.

Living With
an Established Church

The fact that so many countries have established religions doesn't mean that people not belonging to the religion are necessarily persecuted.

But there are some bothersome things. Often the state schools are run by the church and religious study is part of the school program. In England if you are not a member of the Church of England you are called a "dissenter" or a "nonconformist."

In some countries parents are allowed to name their children only from an approved list of names, usually saints' names. If parents wanted to name their son Hercules so he'd grow up very strong it might not be permitted, although if they named him with a saint's name but called him Hercules probably nothing would happen.

The Archbishop of Canterbury stands facing
Queen Elizabeth, after placing the crown on
her head at her coronation.

In some countries there are local cemeteries, but only members of the established religion may be buried in them. In almost all countries with an established religion, part of the tax money would go to support the religion and schools related to it—whether tax-payers approved or not. And in some countries membership in the religion is required of anyone holding public office.

Religious Persecution

Many times, for reasons that really have nothing to do with religion, people are persecuted in the name of religion. A government or group might look for someone to blame for things that have gone wrong in the nation. Or a group belonging to one religion may try to expand its territory or power. Or one religious group may try to show that it is more religious than its neighbors. Although often the established church is not involved in the persecution, equally often the established church does nothing to try to stop it.

The persecution of the Jews under Hitler in Germany during World War II, the centuries-old fighting between Protestants and Roman Catholics in Northern Ireland, the wars between Israel and the Arab nations, and the fighting among various sects of Islam are all examples of how religion can become an excuse for war.

These are terrible, tragic wars and acts, but in most cases religion is the excuse, not the cause. Nevertheless, many people believe a religion, and especially an established religion, has a duty to stop in any way possible such persecutions and that too often it fails to even try.

Chapter

6

Changing Attitudes

Why is separation of church and state so much in the news today? Many people believe it's because the United States is becoming more and more a society with many different points of view on religion.

Where most people are of one religion, few questions come up. In such places even people who don't agree with the dominant religion tend to keep quiet, possibly out of fear, possibly because they think nothing can be changed, or, in liberal countries, because they don't suffer discrimination.

Most conflicts among different religions in the United States have been open. The major religious conflicts were among Protestant groups. These conflicts were anticipated and tempered by Article VI, Section 3, in the Constitution, which states that members of the government should not have to pass any religious test, and by the First Amendment.

Members of other religions who live in the United States, including Roman Catholics, Jews, Jehovah's Witnesses, Mormons, Moslems, and Buddhists, are benefiting today from the early Protestant conflicts. Without early conflict over religion the United

James Madison, "father of the Constitution," was a strong
supporter of separation of church and state.

States might never have established the separation of church and state. Many of the early leaders of our country believed separation of church and state was essential.

One of the best-known early statements on separation of church and state is by James Madison, who has been called the "father of the Constitution." This pamphlet, written in 1785 in opposition to a tax to support teachers of Christianity, is called *Memorial and Remonstrance Against Religious Assessments* and is frequently cited before the Supreme Court.

In it Madison states, "The Religion then of every man must be left to the conviction and conscience of every man; and it is the right of every man to exercise it as these may dictate. . . . We maintain therefore that in matters of Religion, no man's right is abridged by the Institution of Civil Society, and that Religion is wholly exempt from its cognizance. True it is, that no other rule exists, by which any questions which may decide a Society, can be ultimately determined, but the will of the majority; but it is also true, that the majority may trespass on the rights of the minority."

A Protestant Nation

Through most of the eighteenth and nineteenth centuries the United States was a Protestant nation. Since the majority of people shared similar Protestant beliefs—the arguments of the earlier times were more or less forgotten—there was a natural assumption that everyone believed the same things and these beliefs entered into daily life.

When the strong public school movement developed in the nineteenth century, most people saw nothing wrong with Protestant prayers and a Protestant Bible (the King James Version) to start the day—after all, most people were Protestant. As more and more immigrants of other religions came into the country, and especially more Roman Catholics, objections were made to the use of Protestant Bibles and prayers in the public schools. The objections didn't change the practices in the public schools but they did lead to the founding of parochial schools run by the Roman Catholic Church.

It wasn't until 1962 that what was probably the single most dramatic decision relating to religion and the schools was made. Three cases came before the Supreme Court in what are today called "the school prayer cases."

In one case, a school board in New York City, advised to do so by the State Board of Regents (supervisors of education), asked a school principal to have each class say aloud, in front of a teacher, a prayer at the start of each school day.

The prayer was, "Almighty God, we acknowledge our dependence upon Thee, and we beg Thy blessings upon us, our parents, our teachers and our Country."

The prayer was challenged by parents of ten of the students—Ethical Culturists, Jews, Unitarians, and nonbelievers—who said it was contrary to their beliefs. The Supreme Court decided official prayer violated the "establishment" clause in the First Amendment: "Congress shall make no law respecting an establishment of religion. . . ."

Bible Readings

Two later cases, one involving Pennsylvania law, and one involving Maryland law, concerned states where the schools required

Bible readings and the saying of the Lord's Prayer. The cases were brought by parents who were Unitarians and atheists.

Pennsylvania had tried to avoid conflict by using not only the King James Version but also the Revised Standard Version and other versions acceptable to Catholics and Jews; Maryland used the King James Version. In these cases also the Supreme Court decided the readings and prayer violated the "establishment" clause.

Many people who disagree with the decisions to ban prayer from public schools have been trying to find ways to get prayers back into the schools. One of the most obvious ways is with a constitutional amendment. One suggestion was the so-called Becker Amendment, offered by New York Congressman Frank J. Becker.

Although this "amendment" did not become part of the Constitution, it provides an idea of how such an amendment could be written. It says:

Sec. 1. Nothing in this Constitution shall be deemed to prohibit the offering, reading from or listening to prayers or biblical scriptures, if participation therein is on a voluntary basis, in any governmental or public school, institution, or place.

Sec. 2. Nothing in this Constitution shall be deemed to prohibit making reference to belief in, reliance upon, or invoking the aid of God or a Supreme Being in any governmental or public document, proceeding, activity, ceremony, school, institution or place, or upon any coinage, currency, or obligation of the United States.

Sec. 3. Nothing in this article shall constitute an establishment of religion.

The Power of the President
and Presidential Staff

Anyone who wonders about what power President Reagan and his staff may have over the Supreme Court should study what happened in the 1985 Court. The Reagan Administration (through the solicitor general's office, which represents the federal government before the Court) filed legal opinions urging the Court to decide that silent prayer in the schools, guaranteed time off from work to observe a Sabbath, and certain types of public aid to parochial schools were in keeping with the Constitution.

Both the administration and the Court were considered conservative and some people felt there had been signs of the weakening of the "wall" between church and state because of the conservative nature of the Court. Many expected the Court to go along with the administration.

It didn't happen.

In all three cases the Court took the stand opposite to what the administration wanted. The Court said that even silent prayer in the public schools was unconstitutional, that giving guaranteed time off for people to observe their Sabbaths amounted to placing religion above the secular, and that two arrangements whereby public school teachers went into parochial schools to teach were unconstitutional.

The administration had made these three requests in an effort to "get around" certain earlier Court decisions. The decision against silent prayer was a direct result of an attempt to get around the restriction against prayer in the schools. Letting public school teachers teach in parochial schools was an indirect attempt to use federal money in parochial schools, which is against the law.

Even though the administration and the Court were both considered to be conservative, the Court made up its own mind according to the way it saw the Constitution and denied the administration its requests. Each such decision affects the wall of separation and future interpretations of the religion clauses of the First Amendment.

Chapter

7

Future of Separation of Church and State in the United States

What is the future of separation of church and state in the United States? No one knows, but one can guess. Certainly the wall of separation will continue to move one way and then the other as the Supreme Court changes.

For the long term it is impossible to tell what changes will be made in the daily life of the United States as a result of changes in the concept of separation of church and state.

For the short term, however, it is possible to predict what cases will be coming up before the Court.

Christmas and Hanukkah

In 1984 a case was brought to the Court concerning a crèche (nativity scene) Pawtucket, Rhode Island, displayed every Christmas. The question was whether or not it violated separation of church and state, and the Court voted that it did not.

In 1985 a similar case was brought before the Supreme Court concerning Scarsdale, New York. When the Supreme Court voted, the result was a tie (one of the justices was sick), which left the

The crèche in Pawtucket, Rhode Island, which the Supreme Court
decided had not violated separation of church and state.
Opposite: Each year during Hanukkah, the menorah is displayed
in Lafayette Park across from the White House.

previous decision by a lower court standing. The lower court had decided that the village of Scarsdale could not ban a crèche from public land. In other words, the result was similar to that in the Pawtucket case—a crèche did not violate separation of church and state. It's likely more crèche cases will come to the Court.

Because of the attention paid to the crèche cases, other cases related to Christmas may come up.

Many things in American culture connected with Christmas are not really related to Christianity at all, but people think they are. Christmas trees, wreaths, and mistletoe are ornaments and decorations and have nothing to do with the religious aspect of Christmas. Santa Claus has been so changed from the Saint Nicholas he once was as to be unrecognizable.

It seems more than likely that at some point the Supreme Court will have to decide which of the nonreligious symbols of Christmas can be displayed by a municipality without violating the separation of church and state. The question may also be raised as to whether or not displaying a symbol of another religion lessens the religious impact. For example, a symbol of the Jewish religious holiday of Hanukkah, an eight-arched candelabra called a menorah, is displayed at the same time of year as Christmas symbols.

And speaking of Christmas, it is now a national holiday. Should it be?

Thanksgiving

Thanksgiving is likely to prove the most important case—on a par with the school prayer cases—if it ever comes up.

It is a day for giving thanks—and thanks are given to God. Thanksgiving is a day to eat a big traditional meal, but that is certainly not the most important thing about Thanksgiving. Giving thanks is.

It's most unlikely that any person or group that believes in God would question Thanksgiving, but it might be questioned by people who do not believe in God.

Other Cases

Religion tends to be a part of many aspects of life as seen by the courts and by religious groups themselves.

Because of the relationship many people see between morals and religion, certain other matters that touch on religion are likely to come before the Supreme Court in the years ahead. In some cases those bringing the cases will want to overturn previous decisions; in other cases they will want to establish decisions.

Among the cases likely to come up are birth control (prevention of conception by mechanical means), abortion (deliberate removal of the embryo or fetus from the womb before it can live on its own), and homosexuality (sexual relations with someone of one's own sex). Even if these cases are not argued on religious grounds, it seems likely that religious organizations will speak on both sides of these cases if and when they are heard.

What role should religion play in civil government?

This question is taking on new angles as more priests, ministers, and members of religious orders engage in political activity, including running for office. Again, it's likely religion will be heard on both sides of the question.

Cases that have already been decided may come up in a different form, although the Court decides what cases it will hear and usually tends to avoid new cases on recent decisions.

*In forbidding priests to hold public office, the Pope supported
separation of church and state in the United States;
Father Robert Drinan did not seek reelection to Congress in 1980.*

However, there will probably come up more cases concerning such matters as federal aid to parochial schools and the use of federal loan money by students to attend schools with religious affiliation. School prayer isn't going to go away; there are too many people and groups who consider it extremely important for students in the public schools to start the day with prayer.

Many Questions

Someone is likely to challenge the phrase "under God" in the Pledge of Allegiance to the flag. And someone is almost certain to bring up the question of whether or not the fact that our money says on it "In God We Trust" is a violation of separation of church and state.

A case that is well on its way to the Supreme Court deals with the question of after-school clubs. Can a student religious club be permitted under the First Amendment to meet for prayer and discussion on school grounds?

A religious Jew in the armed services feels his religion requires him to wear a head covering even when his commanding officer tells him to take it off. This case, if it reaches the Court, will have widespread implications for other religions including, most dramatically, Sikhism, an Asian religion with a fairly large number of people in the United States. Its followers, called Sikhs, believe their religion requires them to wear a head covering, a turban, at all times.

One of the most interesting cases involves people who have given sanctuary to political refugees from other countries. The government says they are harboring illegal aliens; they say they are practicing their religion. If this case reaches the Court it could give additional definition to separation of church and state.

Many people support while others oppose the right of student religious groups to meet after school on school grounds.

The city of Miami, Florida, employs a person who works as a kosher inspector. Religious Jews won't eat food that isn't kosher—conforming to certain religious laws—but it's very difficult for the consumer to tell if food labeled kosher has been prepared according to the dietary laws.

In Miami, the kosher inspector checks stores, hotels, and restaurants to be sure food sold as kosher is kosher.

Should the city be financing the performance of a religious function?

What Next?

A woman has refused to have her photograph put on her driving license; her religion is one that is strongly against graven images and she believes photographs are graven images.

A father has refused to obtain a Social Security number for his daughter because he believes under his religion that it could be and would be used to rob her of her soul.

These are some of the questions likely to face the Supreme Court concerning separation of church and state. New questions will continue to come up, and various legislatures will continue to pass laws that almost demand challenge.

It's difficult to look far ahead. The Supreme Court does not originate cases. This means that no matter how much the Court would like, say, to decide a case based on whether the phrase "In God We Trust" should continue to be written on money, it must wait for a case concerned with this to make its way up through the courts.

Beyond about the next ten years it's difficult to tell what the feelings of the nation may be.

People may lose interest in "church and state" questions and not bring forth cases involving them. Also, attitudes toward religion tend to change over time. The United States may become more religious—or less religious. The school prayer cases weren't brought forward in the nineteenth century because so many people, including ones who were not religious, accepted the general religious feeling of the period.

And there's no way of telling what a future Supreme Court will be like or will do. The 1985 Court, after all, ignored the advice of the administration and gave liberal decisions when conservative ones were expected.

One thing, however, is certain. The wall of separation between church and state will continue to stand, and will continue to be pushed and pulled now one way and now another.

Chapter

8

Those Important Decisions

It all starts with the Constitution—that's where the rules are first set out that establish separation of church and state as the policy of the United States. Article II permits a president to choose a nonreligious way of taking the oath of office; Article VI states clearly that no religious test can be required of any public official.

The First Amendment to the Constitution forbids Congress from making any laws establishing a religion or interfering with the free exercise of one.

The Fourteenth Amendment extended First Amendment guarantees to actions by the states.

There are almost no limitations to what the religion can be. A person may practice any religion at all—or none. A person may believe anything—or nothing—and is free to do so.

No one can be required to prove that his or her religion is "true" or that he or she honestly believes it. This is the case even when the religion has been accused of fraud (criminal deception).

There are logical limits, of course. If a religion encouraged cannibalism, the government would step in, and rightly so.

Religious beliefs can be carried into seemingly secular situations. Jehovah's Witnesses, believing the American flag is a graven image, refused to salute the flag or permit their children to do so. A Supreme Court case was decided in their favor.

Children may be educated according to their parents' religious beliefs. The state of Oregon required all children through the eighth grade to attend public schools. Parents who wanted their children to attend parochial school took the case to court and won in the Supreme Court.

No one has to take part in a religious ceremony he or she doesn't believe in.

Laws requiring everyone—even those whose Sabbath is Friday or Saturday or whenever—to take Sunday as the Sabbath are unconstitutional.

And the Court recently decided that a law requiring employers to guarantee employees their Sabbath off from work was also unconstitutional.

Public school prayers, whether or not students are forced to take part, are unconstitutional.

Public school teachers may not go into parochial schools to teach subjects such as remedial reading paid for by federal funds.

Problem Cases

Not every Supreme Court decision reflects the detached, judicial, wise attitude that the Court usually presents.

There are two cases in particular that bother some experts.

One case involved the Church of Jesus Christ of Latter Day Saints (Mormons), which at the time (late nineteenth century) was located in the territory of Utah.

The Mormons at that time practiced polygamy (more than one wife per husband), which was encouraged by their religion.

Congress passed a law seizing all property of the Mormon Church (except cemeteries, temples, and parsonages) for sale to raise money for the public schools in Utah because the Mormons practiced polygamy. Congress had this kind of power over Utah because at that time it was a territory, not a state.

Eventually, the Mormon leader announced an end to the practice of polygamy. Not long after, Utah was admitted to the union as a state.

The question: Was the action of Congress in interfering with a religious practice—polygamy—justified by the nature of the practice itself?

The Reverend Sun Myung Moon is the founder of the Unification Church, which may well be the most controversial religious group in recent times.

In addition to saying it isn't a true religion, critics of the Unification Church claim that young people have been trapped into joining the Church by a form of brainwashing.

Many people don't like the fact that the Reverend Mr. Moon is a foreigner, a Korean.

Many people don't like the fact that hundreds of couples (many of whom didn't really know each other) were married by the Church in a mass ceremony at Madison Square Garden in New York. And many people are bothered by what they see as a secretiveness in the Church.

In any case, the Reverend Mr. Moon was charged with income tax evasion (much religious property and income is tax exempt—but it must really belong to the religion) and, in a decision that was upheld by the Supreme Court, was sent to prison for a year.

Controversial though it may be, the Reverend Sun Myung Moon's Unification Church has many adherents.

Some people believe the Reverend Mr. Moon did evade the taxes and deserved to go to jail. Others, however, believe that he didn't go to prison for what he did but because people disliked his form of religion.

These two cases are definite exceptions, and many people believe that the Court was right in both cases. Most of the time, over the years, over changing religious attitudes, Supreme Court decisions on separation of church and state have been ones that most people in the United States have seen as fair interpretations of the Constitution and the First Amendment.

For Further Information

Start by reading the United States Constitution.

Take your time.

You don't have to finish it in one day. Stop reading if your mind is beginning to wander. You can always start again another day.

When you read the Constitution watch for things that are a little surprising to you, possibly because you wouldn't have expected people to think of them in 1791. Try to figure out why those things were included.

Next, read the First Amendment. There's a great deal packed into it in addition to separation of church and state. Again, ask yourself what is being said—and why.

Finish up with the other first nine amendments in the Bill of Rights and you'll have a very good understanding of the legal foundations of our country.

One of the best ways to learn about the Constitution is by learning about some of the people who wrote it. There are biographies available about such influential people as James Madison (who later became president of the United States) and Alexander Hamilton. Reading a biography would introduce you to a very interesting person and give you some idea of the times when the Constitution was written.

Glossary

Administration—the term used to describe the president of the United States and presidential staff. It is also called the executive branch of the government.

Amendment—in terms of the United States Constitution, an addition to the original text.

Bill of Rights—the name given to the first ten amendments to the Constitution. These amendments protect the rights of the individual and the states.

Canon law—church law, especially that of the Roman Catholic Church.

Church—as used in the phrase "separation of church and state," a term referring to any religion, not necessarily a Christian one.

Colleges—in the colonies and later in the early states, institutions formed for higher education of young men, usually with the aim of training ministers.

Colonies—settlements subject to a mother country. The American colonies were subject to Great Britain.

Congregationalists—see Pilgrims.

Conservative—in American politics, a term used to describe a group that wants to keep things as they are; in "church and state" matters this group tends to advocate more rather than less religion in everyday life.

Constitution—a document setting out the basic laws of a country. The United States Constitution is the world's oldest written constitution.

Crèche—a representation, usually life-size, of the stable, manger, Mary and Joseph, animals, and visitors at the birth of Jesus; also called a "nativity scene."

Established church—one considered by the government of a country to be the official church. Often supported by taxes, these churches have varying degrees of power according to where they are situated.

Established religion—the religion practiced by an established church.

"Establishment" clause—the clause of the First Amendment to the United States Constitution that states: "Congress shall make no law respecting an establishment of religion. . . ."

"Free exercise" clause—the clause of the First Amendment to the United States Constitution that states that Congress shall make no law ". . . prohibiting the free exercise" of religion.

Freedom of religion—the right of every individual in a country to worship (or not worship) as he or she pleases. Many countries that have established churches also tolerate freedom of religion.

Lamaseries—monastery-like places in Tibet where lamas (priests or monks of this form of Buddhism) live in some degree of seclusion.

Liberal—in American politics, a term usually referring to people who strongly favor individual freedom and social reform.

Menorah—a candelabra of eight candles burned by Jews on the holiday of Hanukkah in remembrance of when the oil in the Temple lasted a miraculously long time.

Morals—standards of right and wrong sometimes, but not always, related to religion.

Pilgrims—English colonists who sailed on the *Mayflower*, landing at Plymouth, Massachusetts, in 1620. They were Separatists, having broken away from the Church of England.

Preamble—the introduction to the United States Constitution, explaining why it was written.

Puritans—English colonists who landed at Massachusetts Bay in 1630. They were members of the Church of England who believed that the church needed to be reformed, or purified.

Ratify—to approve formally.

Separation of church and state—the ideal expressed in the First Amendment and applied originally to Congress and later to the states through the Fourteenth Amendment. It establishes that government is neither to encourage nor to discourage any religion. The Supreme Court interprets these amendments.

State—in the phrase "separation of church and state," a word meaning "all government."

Supreme Court—the highest court in the United States.

Theocracy—a form of government in which the leaders believe their power comes from a divine being (or beings).

Index